WORKBOOK
FOR

Frankenstein

THE GRAPHIC NOVEL

by Carol Nuttall

HEINLE
CENGAGE Learning

Australia • Brazil • Japan • Korea • Mexico • Singapore • Spain • United Kingdom • United States

HEINLE
CENGAGE Learning

Workbook for Frankenstein
Carol Nuttall

Publisher: Sherrise Roehr

Managing Development Editor: John Hicks

Associate Development Editor: Cécile Engeln

Assistant Development Editor: Heidi North

Director of U.S. Marketing: Jim McDonough

Director of Global Marketing: Ian Martin

Assistant Marketing Manager: Jide Iruka

Director of Production and Media Content:
  Michael Burggren

Associate Content Project Manager:
  Mark Rzeszutek

Print Buyer: Mary Beth Hennebury

Contributing Writer: Neil Bowen

Character Designs & Original Artwork:
  Declan Shalvey

Art Director: Jon Haward

Text Designer: Classical Comics Ltd.

Compositor: MPS Limited, A Macmillan Company

Cover Designer: Gina Petti, Rotunda Design

For product information and technology assistance, contact us at
Cengage Learning Customer & Sales support, 1-800-354-9706

For permission to use material from this text or product,
submit all requests online at **www.cengage.com/permissions**
Further permissions questions can be e-mailed to
permissionrequest@cengage.com

ISBN 13: 978-1-1110-0571-9

ISBN 10: 1-1110-0571-0

Heinle
20 Channel Center Street
Boston, MA 02210
USA

Cengage Learning is a leading provider of customized learning solutions with office locations around the globe, including Singapore, the United Kingdom, Australia, Mexico, Brazil and Japan. Locate our local office at:
international.cengage.com/region

Cengage Learning products are represented in Canada by Nelson Education, Ltd.

Visit Heinle online at **elt.heinle.com**

Visit our corporate website at **www.cengage.com**

CONTENTS

Before You Read

WORKSHEET 1 – MARY SHELLEY

A. Read the brief biography of Mary Shelley on pp. 136–137 of your book and complete the timeline below.

Date	What Happened?
August 30, 1797	
December 30, 1816	
January 1, 1818	
1815–1819	
1822	
1823	
1831	
February 1, 1851	

B. Circle the correct answers to the following questions.

1. Who wrote *A Vindication of the Rights of Woman?*
   a. Mary Shelley   **b.** Mary's father   **c.** Mary's mother

2. Mary met Percy Shelley because of his admiration for _____.
   a. Lord Byron   **b.** her father   **c.** William Wordsworth

3. How did William Godwin feel about his daughter's relationship with Shelley?
   a. he disapproved   **b.** he was very happy   **c.** he did not care

4. How old was Mary when she finished writing *Frankenstein?*
   a. 18   **b.** 20   **c.** 22

5. How many children did Mary give birth to?
   a. three   **b.** four   **c.** five

6. After Percy Shelley died, Mary _____.
   a. remarried   **b.** died soon after   **c.** published her husband's poetry

C. Answer the following questions about Mary Shelley.

1. Why do you think Mary Shelley became a successful writer?

   _____

   _____

2. What inferences would you make about Mary Shelly's personality based on the events of her life?

   _____

   _____

Name _____

WORKSHEET 2 – THE HISTORICAL SETTING OF THE NOVEL

A. Read the text. Then answer the questions that follow.

The French Revolution

Before the French Revolution, France was ruled by Louis XVI. Under his rule, the upper class of French society controlled most of the country's land, money, and power. The upper class lived a life of indulgence and luxury, but the majority of people lived in poverty. People who spoke out against this injustice were often imprisoned in the Bastille, the famous French prison. On July 14, 1789, the people attacked the Bastille. They released the prisoners and took control of the weapons in the prison. This was the beginning of the French Revolution.

The goal of the French Revolution was to bring equality and justice to French society. But the Revolution was also very violent. For example, it became common for peasants to break into the homes of local lords, steal valuables, and kill the lords. In 1793, a new group led by Maximilien Robespierre came to power, and the violence increased. Robespierre was a cruel and angry leader. Anyone who spoke out against his leadership was beheaded by a guillotine. Among the many victims of Robespierre's guillotine was Louis XVI.

While the continual violence caused many thousands of deaths, political power shifted to the common people. A number of large and revolutionary reforms were passed. The upper class was heavily taxed, for example. A bill of rights was also written to protect the people. It protected freedom of speech, of religion, and of the press.

Although the French Revolution was very bloody, in the end, it achieved its aim of bringing greater equality and justice to the people of France.

1. The French Revolution was started by _____.
   a. the upperclass
   b. ordinary people

2. King Louis XVI was killed in 1793 by _____.
   a. having his head cut off
   b. hanging

3. The French leader, Robespierre, was _____.
   a. a strict but fair ruler
   b. cruel and angry

4. The new bill of rights protected _____.
   a. property ownership
   b. freedom of speech, religion, and press

B. Read the paragraph below and fill in the blanks with words from the word bank.

believe	body	create	killed	life	Revolution	scientific	world

Many people 1. _____ that Mary Shelley's writing was influenced by historical events during her lifetime. *Frankenstein* was written in the early 19th century, during a time of 2. _____ discovery. One of the main themes in the novel, the idea of creating 3. _____ from dead material, fascinated people at the time. For example, an Italian scientist named Luigi Galvani put electrical hooks on the body of a criminal who had been 4. _____ by hanging. After the first experiment, Galvani reported that the 5. _____ had shown signs of movement. Galvani's research did not result in anything, but it shows that people believed it might be possible to 6. _____ life. Another theme in the novel is Victor Frankenstein's wish to create a better 7. _____ and to "free people from disease." Many people believe that the way his dream goes so wrong reflects what happened during the French 8. _____ .

C. Answer the questions.

1. What does *galvanize* mean?

_____

2. Write a sentence using the word *galvanize*.

_____

WORKSHEET 3 – THE GOTHIC NOVEL

A. *Frankenstein* is a Gothic novel. Gothic novels are a kind of fiction that was popular in England in the late 18th and early 19th centuries. Gothic novels have the following characteristics:

- they are set in dark, scary places
- they include ghosts or supernatural events
- they often contain romance
- the story features the return of something from the past
- they try to make the reader feel afraid

Research the story of *Dracula* by Bram Stoker. Give reasons why this novel can be classified as Gothic.

_____

_____

_____

_____

_____

B. The Gothic style of writing has become popular again. This can be seen in comic books as well as novels. Name two modern comic books or novels that could be described as Gothic and write a brief description of each.

Modern Gothic Stories	
Title	Description
1.	
2.	

C. *Frankenstein* is the story of a "mad scientist," Victor Frankenstein, whose scientific experiment goes terribly wrong. Can you identify "mad scientists" in the movies *Spiderman* or *The Fantastic Four*? If you have not seen these movies, can you think of another movie or story that includes a "mad scientist"?

_____

_____

_____

_____

D. In pairs, plan a story outline for a Gothic novel or movie. Refer to the list of characteristics in Activity A to help you. Share your ideas with the rest of the class.

Before You Read

WORKSHEET 4 – THE NARRATIVE STRUCTURE

A. Fill in the blanks with words from the word bank.

plot	protagonist	narrator	hero	villain	victim	fate	climax

1. character who tells the story: _____

2. someone who suffers in the story: _____

3. most exciting part of the story: _____

4. the most important person in the story: _____

5. brave, good character in the story: _____

6. evil, bad character in the story: _____

7. a power that some people believe controls what happens: _____

8. the story: _____

B. Several narrators tell the story of *Frankenstein*. The story begins with Captain Robert Walton. Then Victor Frankenstein meets Walton and tells his story to Walton. As the story progresses, it unfolds through different narrators. As the book shifts from one narrator to another, use the flow chart below to take notes about what each narrator reveals and describes.

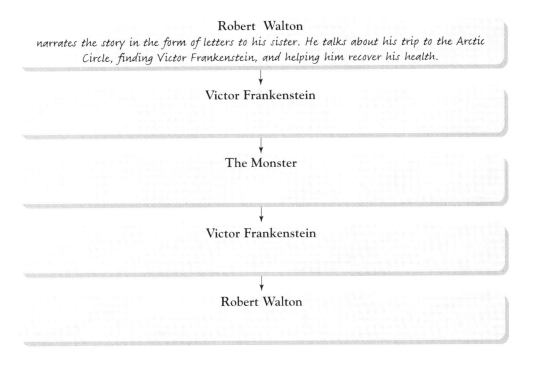

C. Explain the following types of narrators.

1. A narrator who is not a main character:

_____

_____

2. A narrator who is one of the main characters:

_____

_____

Name _____

WORKSHEET 5 – THE PROMETHEUS MYTH

A. Read the text below about the Prometheus myth. Then decide whether the statements that follow are True or False.

> Mary Shelley was influenced by the myth of Prometheus when she wrote *Frankenstein*. The original title for the novel was *Frankenstein: or, The Modern Prometheus*. There are several versions of this myth. The Greek version shows Prometheus as a guardian of humans. In this version, Prometheus feels sorry for humans, and thinks that Zeus, King of the Gods, treats them badly. So Prometheus steals fire from Zeus to give to the humans. Zeus punishes Prometheus cruelly. He has Prometheus chained to a mountain. Each day an eagle eats Prometheus' liver, which then grows back. The later Latin version of the myth has Prometheus creating humans out of clay and water. He is punished for stealing the secret of creation.
>
> *Frankenstein* parallels both versions of the Prometheus myth. Just as the Greek Prometheus steals fire from heaven and gives it to humans. Victor Frankenstein steals the secret of creation and he, too, is punished. *Frankenstein* also clearly parallels the Latin version of the myth. Like the Latin Prometheus, Victor goes against the laws of nature to create life himself. In both the Greek and Latin versions of this myth, Prometheus rebels against the gods or tries to make himself a kind of god by trying to discover the secret of life.

1. *Frankenstein* is a story based on mythology.	True	False
2. There is only one version of the Prometheus myth.	True	False
3. The Greek Prometheus defends humans.	True	False
4. Prometheus steals fire from Zeus for himself.	True	False
5. The Latin Prometheus is someone who wants to have the power to create life.	True	False
6. In both Prometheus myths, Prometheus is punished for his actions.	True	False

B. Answer the questions below.

1. How do we know that Mary Shelly was influenced by the Prometheus myth when she wrote *Frankenstein*?

   _____

   _____

   _____

2. How is Victor similar to Prometheus?

   _____

   _____

   _____

3. Which view do you think Mary Shelley held of the Prometheus Myth? Do you think she saw Prometheus as a defender or creator of humans?

   _____

   _____

   _____

While You Read

WORKSHEET 6 – WALTON'S LETTERS AND VOLUME I, CHAPTERS I-IV

 CD 1 Track 2

A. Listen to the letters that Captain Walton writes to his sister, Margaret. As you listen, complete the following sentences with the correct word or phrase.

Walton is sailing to the 1. _____ and is very excited about his voyage. It is a voyage of discovery. Walton hopes to find the 2. _____ Ocean. However, as he gets nearer to his 3. _____ he feels more and more alone.

One day, the ship is surrounded by 4. _____ and fog. The sailors are surprised to see a sled in the distance. It is being driven by a 5. _____, but the sailors cannot follow him because of the ice.

The next day, the sailors find a man in the sea who floated toward their boat on a piece of ice. The man is extremely thin and almost 6. _____.

After two days, the man is able to speak. The man tells Walton that he is looking for someone who 7. _____ from him. The man tells Walton his story in hopes that Walton may 8. _____ from it.

 CD 1 Tracks 3–5

B. Read and listen to Volume I, Chapters I-III starting on p. 12. Fill in the chart with information about Victor's early life.

Victor Frankenstein

Parents	
Name of his adopted sister	
Name of his friend in Geneva	
Subjects he loves to read about	
Important event at age 15	
Important event at age 17	
Name of his university	

While You Read

WORKSHEET 6 – WALTON'S LETTERS AND
VOLUME I, CHAPTERS I-IV (CONTINUED)

CD 1
Track 6

C. Listen to Volume I, Chapter IV. Decide whether the following statements are True or False. Then read Chapter IV starting on p. 20 to check your answers.

1. Professor Waldman supports Victor's studies.	True	False
2. Victor examines dead bodies to discover the cause of death.	True	False
3. Victor does not learn how to create life.	True	False
4. Victor decides to make the body larger than normal.	True	False
5. Victor becomes very secretive about his work.	True	False

D. Answer the following questions.

1. What is a *quest*?

   _____

   _____

2. Walton and Victor go on quests. Describe their quests.

   a. Walton's Quest:

   _____

   _____

   b. Victor's Quest:

   _____

   _____

   _____

E. Put the following events from Volume I, Chapters I-IV in chronological order.

_____ Victor tells about his boyhood in Naples.

_____ Robert Walton writes his sister to tell her that he has already sailed far from London.

_____ Victor discovers the cause of life.

_____ Victor's mother dies.

_____ The European man, named Victor Frankenstein, takes over the narration.

_____ Walton sees a huge man driving a sled.

_____ Victor is befriended by Monsieur Waldman.

_____ Walton meets and helps save a nearly frozen European man.

_____ Victor tells about his time in Geneva.

_____ Victor leaves for Ingolstadt University.

WhileYou Read

WORKSHEET 7 – VOLUME I, CHAPTERS V-VI

CD 1
Track 7

A. Read along as you listen to Volume I, Chapter V, on p. 22. Use words from the word bank to fill in the chart below with Victor's feelings during each event.

| relief | horror | joy | hope | desperation | confusion |
| excitement | fear | panic | exhaustion | homesickness | |

When Victor is about to bring the Monster to life	
When the Monster starts moving	
When Victor dreams about his dead mother	
When Victor meets Henry Clerval	
When Victor becomes sick	
While Victor recovers from his sickness	

CD 1
Track 8

B. Listen to Volume I, Chapter VI and follow along in your book, starting on p. 35. Then, answer the questions below by circling the letter of the correct answer.

1. In her letter, Elizabeth tells Victor that she is _____ about him.
   a. curious
   b. worried
   c. upset

2. What is the name of the servant Elizabeth talks about in her letter?
   a. William
   b. Justine
   c. Ernest

3. How does Victor feel about Henry Clerval?
   a. ashamed
   b. guilty
   c. grateful

4. How does Victor feel during his time with Henry in the countryside?
   a. indifferent
   b. confused
   c. happy

C. Say whether you agree or disagree with Victor's decisions in Volume I, Chapters V-VI. Check the appropriate box. Be prepared to discuss your answer.

Action	Agree	Disagree
Ran away from the Monster he created		
Didn't tell Henry about the Monster		
Stopped studying science		

While You Read

WORKSHEET 8 – VOLUME I, CHAPTERS VII-VIII

CD 1
Track 9

A. Listen to Volume I, Chapter VII and read along in your book, starting on p. 39. In this chapter, Victor learns three things that shock him. List what shocks Victor and describe his reaction to each one.

1. First Shock: _____

_____

2. Second Shock: _____

_____

3. Third Shock: _____

_____

CD 1
Track 10

B. Read and listen to Volume I, Chapter VIII on p. 48. Then read the summary below and fill in the blanks with words from the word bank.

killed	picture	innocent	murder	truth	guilty

Justine Moritz is accused of William's 1. _____ . William was wearing a necklace with his mother's 2. _____ in a locket when he was killed. It was found in Justine's pocket. Justine says she doesn't know how the necklace got in her pocket. The court decides she is 3. _____ . Victor and Elizabeth visit her and learn that she has confessed. Justine tells them that she lied and that she is really 4. _____ . Justine tells Elizabeth that she is not afraid to die. But she wants the Frankenstein family to know the 5. _____. The next day, Justine is 6. _____ .

C. Why do you think Victor does not tell everyone about the Monster in order to save Justine? List three possible reasons below.

1. _____

2. _____

3. _____

D. Imagine William's murder has just happened. You are police officers investigating his death. What evidence are you looking for at the crime scene? What questions are you asking? Do you think Justine Moritz is going to be found guilty of William's murder?

_____

_____

_____

_____

While You Read

WORKSHEET 9 – VOLUME II, CHAPTERS I-III

A. Listen to Volume II, Chapters I-III with your books closed. Decide whether the following statements are True or False.

CD 1
Tracks
11–13

1. Victor goes into the mountains to find the Monster.	True	False
2. When Victor sees the Monster, he wants to kill him.	True	False
3. The Monster tries to kill Victor.	True	False
4. The Monster believes that Victor should help him.	True	False
5. The Monster asks Victor to listen to his story.	True	False
6. Victor feels a responsibility to make the Monster happy.	True	False
7. The Monster says that he was good, but unhappiness made him bad.	True	False
8. Villagers attacked the Monster when he came near them, and he ran away.	True	False
9. The Monster found shelter in a small hut next to where a family lived.	True	False
10. Watching the family's kindness gave the Monster new feelings.	True	False

B. Listen to Volume II, Chapters I-III again and follow along starting on p. 52. Circle words from the list below that describe the Monster.

CD 1
Tracks
12–13

strong	dangerous	violent	sad	smart
weak	lonely	happy	wild	

C. Re-read Volume II, Chapters II-III starting on page 52. In these chapters, Victor has his first real meeting with his creation. Use the chart below to compare how Victor and the Monster feel about each other. Use the words in the word bank and your own words.

anger	bitterness	horror	fear	disappointment
disgust	guilt	desperation	responsibility	sadness

How Victor feels about the Monster	How the Monster feels about Victor

D. Victor describes his creation as a "Monster." Why do you think Victor does not give the Monster a name? How do you think the Monster feels about not having a name?

_____

_____

_____

While You Read

WORKSHEET 10 – VOLUME II, CHAPTERS IV-VIII

A. Listen to Volume II, Chapters IV-V and read along in your book starting on p. 61. What does the Monster learn from watching the people in the cottage? Make a list of four things he learns.

CD 1
Tracks
14–15

1. _____

2. _____

3. _____

4. _____

B. Listen to Volume II, Chapter VI as you read along on p. 67. Explain why the De Lacey family was sent away from France.

CD 1
Track 16

_____

_____

C. Listen to Volume II, Chapters VII-VIII. A series of events cause the Monster to become bad. Complete the diagram below to show what happens to the Monster.

CD 1
Tracks
17–18

6. He is angry and goes to find Victor. On the way, he _____ _____.

1. The Monster is kind to the family in the cottage and wants _____ _____.

5. On his way to Geneva, he rescues a drowning girl and is _____ _____.

2. When the Monster meets the blind man, the man _____ _____.

4. The Monster becomes so upset that he _____ _____.

3. When the rest of the family comes home and sees the Monster, they _____ _____.

While You Read

WORKSHEET 10 – VOLUME II, CHAPTERS IV-VIII (CONTINUED)

D. Victor's Monster has both good qualities and bad qualities. Name some of the Monster's good and bad qualities in the chart below.

Good Qualities	Bad Qualities

CD 1
Track 18

E. Listen to Volume II, Chapter VIII as you read along on p. 73. Complete the following sentences about the events that lead to the Monster's first murder.

pocket	Frankenstein	friend	burns	shoots	screams

1. After the family rejects him, the Monster _____ their cottage.
2. When the Monster saves a little girl's life, her father _____ him.
3. The Monster sees young William in the woods and tries to make William his _____.
4. William fights the Monster and _____.
5. When the Monster realizes that the boy is a _____, he kills him.
6. The Monster sees Justine sleeping in a barn and puts William's picture in her _____.

Name _____

CD 1
Tracks
18–19

A. With your book closed, listen to Volume II, Chapter VIII again. Then listen to Chapter IX. Make a list of six important events that occur in these chapters. Make sure the events are listed in the order in which they happen.

_____

_____

_____

_____

_____

_____

B. Now read Volume II, Chapters VIII-IX, starting on p. 73. The chart below lists three of the Monster's actions. List a reason for each of these actions.

Monster's Action	Reason
Asks Victor to make a female monster to be with him	
Murders William	
Makes Justine look guilty for murdering William	

C. Check whether you Agree or Disagree with the actions below. Then explain why. Be prepared to discuss your answers.

Action	Disagree	Agree	Why?
1. The Monster murders William.			
2. The Monster makes Justine look guilty.			
3. The Monster asks Victor to make a female monster.			
4. Victor refuses to create another monster.			
5. The Monster promises to leave forever if Victor creates a female monster for him.			
6. Victor promises to create a female monster.			

D. Do you think Victor and the Monster are completely evil? Do you feel any sympathy for them? Why or why not?

_____

_____

_____

_____

_____

_____

WORKSHEET 12 – VOLUME III, CHAPTERS I-II

A. Listen to Volume III, Chapters I-II with your books closed. Put a check next to any information you hear.

CD 2
Tracks
2–3

1. _____ Victor returns home and forgets about the Monster.
2. _____ Victor still wants to marry Elizabeth.
3. _____ Victor knows he cannot get married until he makes a mate for the Monster.
4. _____ Victor wants to get married immediately.
5. _____ Victor decides to go to England to do his work.
6. _____ Victor's father asks Henry to go with him.
7. _____ Henry and Victor look for different things during their trip to London.
8. _____ Victor does not think the Monster is following him.
9. _____ Victor goes to a Scottish island to be alone and finish his work.
10. _____ Victor loves his work.

Now read Volume III, Chapters I-II starting on p. 84 to check your answers.

B. Listen to Volume III, Chapter II and follow along in your book starting on p. 87. Circle the words that best describe Henry's character.

CD 2
Track 3

| social | busy | quiet | happy | interested | bored | friendly | loyal | kind | sad |

C. Answer the following questions.

1. As Victor gets ready to make another monster, how does he feel? What worries him?

_____

_____

_____

2. How is Victor different from his friend, Henry?

_____

_____

_____

3. Why does Victor travel to an island where there are not many people?

_____

_____

_____

While You Read

WORKSHEET 13 – VOLUME III, CHAPTERS III-IV

CD 2
Track 4

A. Listen to Volume III, Chapter III and read along in your book on p. 92. Victor thinks about what might happen if he makes a female monster. List some of the fears that make him decide not to create another monster.

1. _____
_____

2. _____
_____

3. _____
_____

4. _____
_____

5. _____
_____

6. _____
_____

B. Describe how the Monster reacts when Victor ruins his female monster. Use some of the following words to help you.

| horrified | angry | upset | sad | furious | vengeful |

_____
_____
_____

CD 2
Track 5

C. Listen to Volume III, Chapter IV and read along in your book on p. 102. Answer the following questions.

1. Why do the Irish accuse Victor of murder?

_____
_____

2. Who was murdered?

_____
_____

3. How does Victor react to this murder?

_____
_____

4. Why do you think the judge, Mr. Kirwin, helps Victor?

_____
_____

5. Why does the court decide that Victor is innocent of the murder?

_____
_____

Name _____

A. Listen to Volume III, Chapters V-VI and read along in your book starting on p. 107. Read the summary below. Fill in the blanks with words from the word bank.

CD 2
Tracks
6–7

| destroy | dies | nervous | scream | marries | neck | knife | Monster |

> Victor returns to Geneva with his father. He 1. _____ Elizabeth, even though he is worried about the Monster's threat. For protection, he carries a gun and a 2. _____ . He and Elizabeth are very happy.
>
> The night of his wedding, Victor becomes very 3. _____ . He sends Elizabeth to bed alone. He thinks that the 4. _____ will come to kill him. Then he hears a 5. _____ from upstairs and realizes that he made a terrible mistake. He rushes upstairs. He finds Elizabeth dead, with the Monster's finger marks on her 6. _____ . Victor sees the Monster and shoots at him, but the Monster escapes.
>
> The news of Elizabeth's death affects Victor's father badly, and he 7. _____ soon after.
>
> Victor talks to a judge. He asks the judge to help him find the Monster. The judge says it would be too hard. Victor decides to 8. _____ the Monster himself.

B. Complete the following sentences.

1. Victor thinks the Monster is going to kill him because _____.
2. Even though the Monster made a threat about Victor's wedding night, Victor decides
   to _____.
3. Victor sends Elizabeth to bed so that he can _____.
4. The Monster kills Elizabeth because _____.
5. The judge tells Victor that he cannot _____.

C. Answer the following questions.

1. Why does the Monster kill Elizabeth?

_____

_____

2. Why does the Monster let Victor live?

_____

_____

3. Why does Victor want to destroy the Monster?

_____

_____

WORKSHEET 15 – VOLUME III, CHAPTER VII

A. How do you think the story will end? Write your prediction in the lines below.

_____

_____

_____

CD 2
Track 8

B. Listen to Volume III, Chapter VII and follow along on p. 116. Decide which character said each quote below. Write *Walton*, *Victor*, or *Monster* on the lines.

1. "Let him feel the dreadful sadness that I feel!"   _____

2. "He left messages on trees or stones to guide me."   _____

3. "Learn from my mistakes, and don't make yourself
   completely miserable."   _____

4. "My crazy schemes may be the cause of our deaths."   _____

5. ". . . I felt both interested in him and sorry for him." _____

6. ". . . I cannot believe that I am the same creature
   that at one time wanted only beauty and goodness."   _____

C. Answer the following questions.

1. Where does Victor travel while following the Monster?

_____

_____

2. Why does Victor "fear death"?

_____

_____

3. How does the Monster feel when Victor dies?

_____

_____

While You Read

WORKSHEET 15 – VOLUME III, CHAPTER VII (CONTINUED)

D. Regret is an important theme in *Frankenstein*. Victor and the Monster both regret things that they did. Name two things that each character regrets doing.

Victor

_____

_____

_____

The Monster

_____

_____

_____

_____

E. At the end of the story, Walton meets the Monster. Answer the following questions about their meeting.

1. How does Walton react to the Monster?

_____

_____

2. How is Walton's reaction different from Victor's?

_____

_____

3. What does this tell us about Walton's character?

_____

_____

4. Why does Walton let the Monster leave?

_____

_____

5. Why does the Monster say he is going to burn himself?

_____

_____

After You Read

WORKSHEET 16 – KNOWLEDGE AND RESPONSIBILITY

A. Answer the following questions in the chart below.

1. What knowledge do Victor and the Monster gain in the novel?
2. How does this knowledge give them power?
3. Do Victor and the Monster take responsibility for their actions?

	Victor	**The Monster**
1. Knowledge	He learns how to create life.	
2. Power		
3. Responsibility		

B. Why do you think Victor destroys the female monster? What is he afraid might happen?

_____

_____

_____

_____

_____

Name _____

WORKSHEET 17 – THE MONSTER: EVIL BY NATURE?

A. The Monster has both a good side and an evil side. In the chart below, write examples of his good side and his evil side from the story.

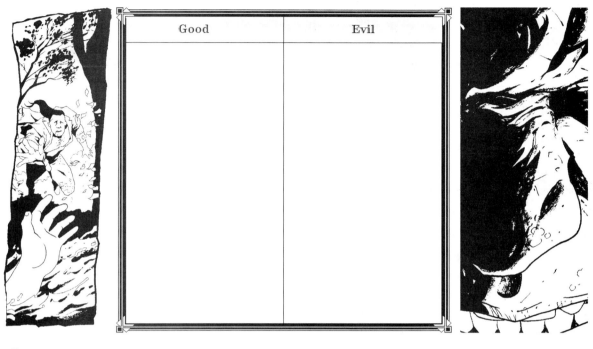

Good	Evil

B. Answer the following questions.

1. Why does Victor reject the Monster? Do you think Victor's rejection of the the Monster makes the situation worse?

   _____

   _____

   _____

2. Why do people run away from the Monster? How important do you think appearance is?

   _____

   _____

   _____

C. Pretend that you are the Monster. You have just learned to read, write, and speak. You have read Victor's notes on his experiments. Write a letter to Victor telling him about yourself. Ask him questions about why he made you and then ran away from you.

_____

_____

_____

_____

_____

_____

_____

Name _____

WORKSHEET 18 – ELIZABETH AND HENRY CLERVAL

A. Answer the following questions about Elizabeth and Henry.

  1. A stereotype is an image that we have of a group of people. Do you think Elizabeth is a believable character, or does she seem like a stereotype of a weak woman?

_____

_____

_____

  2. Henry is a loyal friend to Victor. When Victor is sick or depressed, Henry helps him recover. Why do you think Victor does not tell him about the Monster?

_____

_____

_____

  3. Both Elizabeth and Henry are caring and loyal companions to Victor. Victor acts strangely and does not talk to them for a long time, but they are still his faithful friends. What is their role in the story?

_____

_____

_____

B. An unconditional friend is someone who is still your friend no matter what you say or do. List three examples that show how Henry is an unconditional friend to Victor.

  1. _____

_____

  2. _____

_____

  3. _____

_____

C. Someone who has unconditional love is someone who loves you even when you make mistakes. List three examples of Elizabeth's unconditional love for Victor.

  1. _____

_____

  2. _____

_____

  3. _____

_____

After You Read

WORKSHEET 19 – BOOK REVIEW

A. Write a book review of *Frankenstein: The Graphic Novel*. A book review discusses a book's strengths and weaknesses. Answer the following questions in your book review.
  • Was the book interesting?
  • Did the pictures help you understand what was happening?
  • What was your favorite part of the story?
  • What didn't you like about the story?
  • How did you feel about the characters?
  • What did you learn?
  • Would you recommend this book to other students? Why?

_____

_____

_____

_____

_____

_____

_____

_____

_____

_____

_____

_____

_____

_____

_____

_____

_____

_____

_____

_____

_____

_____

_____

_____

_____

_____

B. Exchange book reviews with a partner. After you read each other's reviews, discuss the book and what you thought about it.

After You Read

WORSHEET 20 – ACT IT OUT!

A. An important part of a film or theater production is the setting. The setting is important in creating the right mood for the events that are about to happen. In *Frankenstein*, the action takes place in several settings. Put the list of settings in the correct order. Some may be used more than once.

England	Geneva	Ingolstadt University (Frankenstein's workshop)	Walton's ship
Orkney Island, Scotland		woods where the Monster lives	hut by Felix's cottage

1. Walton's ship _____   6. _____
2. _____   7. _____
3. _____   8. _____
4. _____   9. _____
5. _____   10. _____

B. With a small group, pick a chapter of *Frankenstein: The Graphic Novel* to act out. Work with your group to fill in the chart.

Volume and Chapter:	
Setting:	
Characters:	
Actors:	
Narrator:	

While you practice with your group, think about:

- The position of the actors and their movements during the scene.
- The facial expressions each character makes in each part of the scene.
- Speaking loudly and clearly enough so that an audience can hear and understand the actors.

After rehearsing your scene, act it out for the class.

Name _____

OPTIONAL FILM WORKSHEET – *FRANKENSTEIN* FILM

A. Watch a film version of *Frankenstein*. As you watch the film, compare it with the book. Make notes in the chart below.

	Same	**Different**
Beginning of the story		
Victor		
The Monster		
Elizabeth		
Justine		
Henry		
Robert		
Felix and family		
Development of plot		
Ending		

B. Answer the questions about the film version of *Frankenstein*.

1. Is anything from the book missing in the film? Do you think the missing parts change the story in a good or bad way?

_____

_____

_____

_____

2. What was your favorite part of the film?

_____

_____

_____

_____

3. What did you enjoy more, the book or the film? Explain your choice.

_____

_____

_____

_____

APPENDIX

Mary Shelley's Works

1819	*Mathilda*
1823	*Valperga*
1826	*The Last Man*
1830	*The Fortunes of Perkin Warbeck*
1835	*Lodore*
1837	*Falkner*
1844	*Rambles in Germany and Italy*

Mary Shelley also wrote many short stories, essays, poems, and reviews that were published in journals and magazines, such as *London Magazine* and *Westminster Review*.

APPENDIX

Extra Resources

Frankenstein

http://www.gutenberg.org/files/84/84.txt

Mary Shelley

http://www.literaryhistory.com/19thC/SHELLEYM.htm
http://www.online-literature.com/shelley_mary/

Victorian Literature and Culture

http://www.victorianweb.org/